CUSTOMER SERVICE SECRETS

THE MOST EFFECTIVE BUSINESS STRATEGY OF ALL IS A SATISFIED CUSTOMER.

BY

SHEALTIEL E. SOLOMON

Copyright © by Shealtiel E. Solomon 2022. All rights reserved.

Before this document is duplicated or reproduced in any manner, the publisher's consent must be gained. Therefore, the contents within can neither be stored electronically, transferred, nor kept in a database. Neither in Part nor full can the document be copied, scanned, faxed, or retained without approval from the publisher or creator.

TABLE OF CONTENT

CUSTOMER SERVICE SECRETS	1
TABLE OF CONTENT	3
Chapter 1	5
WHO IS A CUSTOMER?	5
Chapter 2	12
WHAT IS CUSTOMER SERVICE?	12
Chapter 3	24
CUSTOMER SERVICE QUALITIES.	24
Chapter 4	36
CUSTOMER LOYALTY.	36
Chapter 5	46
SALES OBJECTION.	46
Chapter 6	64
CUSTOMER RETENTION	64
Chapter 7	78
COMMUNICATION AND RAPPORT.	78
Chapter 8	85
THE PROCESS OF CLOSURE.	85
Chapter 9	95
TROUBLESHOOTING AND ESCALATION.	95
Chapter 10	110
ENGAGEMENT OF THE CUSTOMER.	110
Chapter 11	127
HEALTH AND SAFETY OF CUSTOMERS.	127
Chapter 12	138
SELF-EVALUATION IN CUSTOMER SERVICE.	138
Chapter 13	160
POLICY FOR CUSTOMER SERVICE.	160
SUMMARY.	172

The most effective business strategy of all is a satisfied customer.

The most effective business strategy of all is a satisfied customer.

Chapter 1

WHO IS A CUSTOMER?

A customer is a recipient of goods, services, products, or ideas - obtained from a seller, vendor, or supplier via a financial transaction or exchange for a payment or some other valuable consideration. In sales, a customer is the beneficiary of goods, services, products, or ideas offered by a seller, vendor, or supplier via a financial transaction or any other criteria. Services, care, and relationship management inclusive have a direct impact on a customer.

Services are a helpful technique for providing specific responses to specific requests.

Care entails exerting a significant level of compassion or connection, associating a value with something, and demonstrating interest in a person or task to reduce risks or losses.

The most effective business strategy of all is a satisfied customer.

Relationship management is the act of maintaining interpersonal and beneficial contact with people or tasks.

Customers are there to fully accept your offer and to help a business or brand produce cash, thus they require the following;
- Service (a valuable activity).
- Care (deep attention).
- Relationship (effective communication).

You need these skills if you want to succeed as a customer service representative, strategist, coach, or upcoming expert.

These skills will aid in your regular dealings with your customers. They are not limited to soft skills and computer skills. These skills include leadership, communication, innovation, multitasking, time management, teamwork, and problem-solving.

The most effective business strategy of all is a satisfied customer.

In the process of reading, you will encounter a variety of customer types.

Do you find yourself easily irritated? If so, you must be as calm as a dove. Yes! Calm because you are a problem solver, not a problem hardener. If an unsatisfied customer comes in, you should acknowledge and accept that the customer is not angry with you, but with the company or brand. So, relax and respond to such customers.

You must maintain emotional control even if you are not in a good mood. The willingness to give extraordinary service even in difficult situations is what makes customer service excellent.

CUSTOMER TYPES

There are numerous types of customers, however, these three are fairly common. They are:

1. The outspoken customer
2. The passive customer
3. The perturbed customer

OUTSPOKEN CUSTOMER.

Outspoken customers are customers that know exactly what they want and how to get it done respectfully and calmly without being overbearing. You must be cautious when using words with such a customer because they may report your misconduct if they are offended.

PASSIVE CUSTOMERS

Passive customers are customers who are unaware of what they are seeking. These customers might not even understand they are at fault unless you explain it to them. Even after you have explained everything to them, they will still indicate the intention of switching to another company.

Such customers are more inclined to convert from your brand to a competitor. As a result, you must teach them and monitor their growth.

The most effective business strategy of all is a satisfied customer.

PERTURBED CUSTOMER.

Perturbed customers are customers that will help their displeasure with you. They may not allow you to make a welcoming note or glad tidings.

You ought to know that these customers are depressed about an issue and need it settled. Some customer service professionals prefer perturbed customers because they are more likely to speak up when a problem
arises than passive customers who would rather keep quiet and go to a rival. Additionally, it can be challenging to win back an angry customer on occasion if you lose one due to your negligence.

How to treat a perturbed customer.

Your technique of correspondence and approach to your customer is vital. You can use the following techniques:

1. Resist the desire to panic.
2. Listen intently to the customer.

The most effective business strategy of all is a satisfied customer.

3. Repeat back what the customers have said.

4. Thank the customer for drawing your attention to the issue.

5. Utilize accessible programs to confirm the cases of the customer.

6. Make sense of the techniques you will take to determine the issue.

7. If required, make an opportunity to circle back to them.

8. Be clear and honest with them regarding the most usual manner of settling the issue. Give them the usual organization target period if they request a specific time and avoid making promises about things that are beyond your realm of experience.

There is only one boss in each sphere of business. He can choose to recruit and fire the organization.

The most effective business strategy of all is a satisfied customer.

This is because the customer can choose to channel his buying ability to another contender.

If there is no customer, there is no business. The customer's satisfaction is our priority in all we do, in every concept we have, in every innovation we develop, and with every partner, we work with.

THE CUSTOMER IS THE BOSS.

The most effective business strategy of all is a satisfied customer.

Chapter 2

WHAT IS CUSTOMER SERVICE?

Customer service is the provision of high-quality goods or services that satisfy a customer's needs and spark their interest.

Customer service must maintain customer loyalty to prevent customers from switching to a competing brand.
No matter how high you may regard your products as being of the finest quality and inaccessible elsewhere, back them up with EXCELLENT CUSTOMER SERVICE.

Components in customer service.
There is a distinction between giving your customers what they specifically need and making them happy and giving them what they specifically need but making them miserable since your customer's feelings must also be satisfied.

The most effective business strategy of all is a satisfied customer.

There are three key components in Customer service;

1. The service
2. The customer
3. The approach

1. The Service.

At the point when you interact with your customer, it is vital to note the point of not just simply delivering the customer the expected quality however but fulfilling the customer in addition. The choice to depart from your business' premises content and be happy should be available to your customer. A happy customer will always make a purchase and provide customer recommendations.

2. The Customer

A customer is somebody who gives money to you, an establishment, or a brand in exchange for goods or services.

The most effective business strategy of all is a satisfied customer.

Customers should feel satisfied that they have paid for a service or item and received it by their expectations and follow through on a reasonable rate for quality services or products.

At whatever moment they enter, they need someone who will recognize their needs and help them highlight them. They need somebody to hold their hands and take them through a procedure. Customer service begins with the ability to pay attention to the customer and determine what he or she needs through friendly conversation. Each business should treat the customer appropriately.

The idea behind constant customer service is that it is meant to address whatever issues the customer may have. Contact and customer service imply that the customers will be heard and that issues won't be disregarded. It also means getting to know your customer, his or her likes and dislikes, and opinions. The other most crucial part to undertake is to pay attention to what the customer is talking about.

The most effective business strategy of all is a satisfied customer.

3. The Approach.

This phrase means that you should prioritize serving your customers above all else. This is regarded as being "customer-friendly". This technique is popular among most firms or organizations that provide good customer service. Such companies use this approach to establish a system and attitude that encourages customer-friendly service.

This welcoming environment for customers is the source of the proverb "The customer is always right."

WHY IS CUSTOMER SERVICE IMPORTANT?

Customer Service is important for a variety of reasons some of which are listed below:

1. It assists you in withholding clients.

On the off chance that a customer has a decent involvement in an organization, they're bound to return, and the more faithful customers you have, the more your organization can develop to its maximum capacity.

The most effective business strategy of all is a satisfied customer.

For example, assuming that your customer care group has a consistent strategy that makes online returns fast and straightforward, you're bound to hold customers and construct an unwavering customer base that values your no-bother merchandise exchange.

2. It increases staff retention

Staff desire to work for organizations that treat their customers decently. At the point when your workers see that your organization is centered around conveying extraordinary customer service, they will be bound to become advocates for the business. They are likewise undeniably bound to stay with the organization and be completely attached to their work.

3. It supports organizational/brand values.

Your customer support group speaks with customers day to day which implies that they are straightforwardly liable for addressing your brand's main goal and values.

The most effective business strategy of all is a satisfied customer.

Extraordinary customer service can bring about certain surveys and informal exchange suggestions for your business that can prompt new business. A positive public persona can reinforce how individuals see your organization, items, or administration.

Extraordinary customer service can bring about certain surveys and informal exchange suggestions for your business that can prompt new business. A positive public persona can reinforce how individuals see your organization, items, or administration.

4. It generates references.

Positive informal exchange references come straightforwardly from past and existing customers that have had an extraordinary involvement in your organization. They tell their companions, family members, and associates and may try to post to their informal community about your well-disposed sportive customer service. Their contacts, thus, feel urged to purchase from you. Verbal exchange publicizing is many times an organization's ideal and most economical type of promotion.

The most effective business strategy of all is a satisfied customer.

5. It improves Customer Lifetime Value.

Customer lifetime value (CLV) addresses the aggregate sum of income your organization can hope to get from a secluded customer in the long run.

By expanding the CLV, you can essentially build your organization's income without spending more on showcasing. A rising CLV implies that your clients are investing more cash for the energy they request or they are purchasing on a more regular basis.

Customer service is an incredible method for expanding CLV. On the off chance that customers have a positive shopping experience, they'll be bound to purchase from you once more. Showcasing new items to existing customers is likewise simpler. Return customers are bound to believe the products and services your customer service group is suggesting because previously they had an extraordinary encounter.

6. It proactively handles customer problems.

Proactive customer service is when you reach out to customers before they know that problems exist.

The most effective business strategy of all is a satisfied customer.

By being proactive with your customer service strategy, you can let customers know that you're working to improve their user experience for them.

For instance, if you have a faction of customers who had a mutual problem and released a new product or feature that deciphered that issue, you could use your ticketing strategy to identify those customers and then reach out to let them know about the new feature or service. This method can be effective because customers realize you're trying to decipher problems for them.

7. It gives you a strong advantage.

Great customer service fulfills more than just winning over new customers and retaining loyal ones. It also sets you apart from the competition. By proposing best-in-class customer service, you are connecting value to your brand, maintaining your prestige in the market place and demonstrating by example that you care about the people who purchase your product or service.

The most effective business strategy of all is a satisfied customer.

BENEFITS OF CUSTOMER SERVICE.

1. Produces Repeat Patronage.

One of the main benefits of good customer service is that it persuades people to do business with your brand more than once. Repeat sales are not spontaneous, and without building an optimistic customer experience, buyers will go elsewhere. One of the benefits of good customer service is that it creates an emotional rapport with your target audience.

When you treat customers with compassion and affection, you create a connection that makes your customers hesitant to go elsewhere with their business. But the advantages of good customer service don't just stop during a bargain, whether on the phone or in person. By taking a step further such as sending a thank-you email after each purchase, you substantiate the value of buyers regardless of the amount of their purchase.

The most effective business strategy of all is a satisfied customer.

2. Reinforces Business Reputation

Improving your brand's reputation is another example of the benefits of good customer service. Customers often chatter about their experience when dealing with businesses or brands, particularly if it's seldom good or bad. By providing strong customer service, you're making use of the effective marketing tool known as word-of-mouth advertising as I stated earlier. Customers will be delighted to tell their colleagues and relatives about how well your brand has handled them, resulting in more advertising that doesn't cost you anything.

3. Provides a Competitive Edge.

What sets you apart from the competition? Sure, you might provide slightly different goods or services, but unless you're making an incredible, exceptional offer, you should still stand to gain from providing good customer service. In a time when customers often complain about the lack of service or the feeling that they mean little to a brand, delivering excellent customer service can set you apart from your competitors.

The most effective business strategy of all is a satisfied customer.

By intensifying customer service in your marketing strategy and then backing it up, you'll set yourself apart from companies that don't deliver on their promises, creating a sense of uniqueness about your brand.

4. Enhances Employee Capacity.

The benefits of good customer service can also influence the kind of work environment you create at your company. Your staff will feel more strongly aligned with the values and tenets upon which your business was built if they observe that you place a high priority on customer service and everything that it entails, including respect for others, kindness, and going above and beyond. This can lead to a more pleasant environment and make employees feel good about what they do.

5. Contends Higher Rates.

As a small company, you simply may not be able to afford to offer the low prices that the corporate chain stores around the corner charge.

The most effective business strategy of all is a satisfied customer.

One of the unspoken advantages of strong customer service is that by offering a superior customer experience, you may more than makeup for your higher rates. When your business has earned the reputation of offering top-notch customer service, you have the freedom to charge more for your goods and services because customers are willing to pay more to feel appreciated and wanted.

The most effective business strategy of all is a satisfied customer.

Chapter 3

CUSTOMER SERVICE QUALITIES.

It is important to stress the professional aspects of customer service that are always related to the needs of the consumer.

Although there are many different customer needs, these six fundamentals stand out:

1. Friendship, which is the most fundamental quality and is related to decency and politeness. No matter how annoying, loud, or intolerable a client is, you must still have a customer-friendly stance.

2. Empathy — The customer must feel that the service provider understands their demands and situation. It's as simple as putting yourself in your customers' shoes and experiencing their feelings by letting them know you understand them. If you have had similar experiences in the past, you may even tell them.

3. Fairness - The customer wants to believe that they are given sufficient attention and logical responses.

4. Control - The customer wants to feel that his or her preferences and involvement have an impact on the result.

5. Information - Customers expect information about goods and services, but it needs to be timely and relevant.

6. Product knowledge – Customer service representatives must be knowledgeable about the goods or services they offer.

The most effective business strategy of all is a satisfied customer.

When a service provider responds, "I don't know" or "It is not my department," the customer automatically denigrates and demotes them. These workers may come to feel aggressive and underqualified. Customers desire information, and they treat the individual who should have it but doesn't with contempt and mistrust.

How to make a good impression right away.

Here are several strategies for creating favorable impressions, some of which have been proactively used.

- Being mindful when attending to the customer's needs
- Generosity
- Neatness
- Sincere smile
- Moral responsibility relating to a customer
- Quick critical thought for the client
- Providing prompt aid

The most effective business strategy of all is a satisfied customer.

- A pleasant voice tone
- Bringing up the customer's name during a conversation
- Respectful and considerate behavior

Several things can leave a bad or unfavorable impression, including:

- Causing the customer to pause
- Not answering the phone right away
- Not using the words "please" or "thank you"
- Speaking loudly or in a dismissive manner to clients or partners
- Having messy hair or appearing careless with your look
- An awkward handshake
- Making a sarcastic gesture
- Sincere and truthful absence
- Squinting, acting distant, making expressions, and not beaming

The most effective business strategy of all is a satisfied customer.

- Concentrating on completing one last errand while attending to or overhauling a customer.

INCREASING CUSTOMER SATISFACTION.

"Dress as you would like to be addressed" is a proverb. Even though this won't result in the ideal level of customer satisfaction, maintaining a professional appearance is wise for business. Your appearance, facial and hand movements, as well as the content of what you have to say, should all be improved by the way you dress, the impression you make, and what you have to say. It turns out that being persuasive and affecting perception involves more than just the content.

Remember that a person's words and actions should always take precedence over whether or not they are well-groomed, smiling, or well-attired.

However, how you appear has a big impact on how people perceive you and react to you.

PERSONAL CHARACTERISTICS THAT AFFECT CONSUMER SATISFACTION

• Your appearance - how you present yourself to your customer matters a lot. Poor dressing, untidy hair, and dirty hands can turn away a consumer who would otherwise be pleased. Dress cleanly and professionally when talking with customers to command respect and convey that you take your job seriously.

• Smiling - nothing welcomes a customer better than a grin and a friendly face, especially if the consumer has a complaint. An irritated consumer can be quickly calmed down with a smile and friendly talk. Before you even start speaking, a happy facial expression establishes the mood.

The most effective business strategy of all is a satisfied customer.

Most of the time, a calm or pleasing facial expression is desirable.

• Maintain eye contact with your customers at all times. Address customers directly.

• Shaking hands - A solid and professional handshake is expected when shaking hands with a consumer. In a professional setting, both men and women now use this component of greeting.

• Pay attention; when you are listening to a customer, bend slightly in their direction and nod your head slightly to show that you are paying attention.

• Posture: When talking with a customer, slumping in your chair or leaning against a wall are telltale signals that you are uninterested in them. openness and kindness.

The most effective business strategy of all is a satisfied customer.

To convey your interest to the consumer, lean forward, turn to face them, and nod.

• Tone of speech - Customers might occasionally be annoying or challenging. Never, under any circumstance, shout in rage or exasperation. Always come across as friendly.

• Hand motions – emphasize what you say and your feelings by using hand gestures, even when speaking on the phone.

• Personal space is the space between you and another person that you find to be comfortable. When someone approaches you and enters your personal space, you should immediately and thoughtlessly go back. To make customers feel safe and secure, there needs to be enough room.

The most effective business strategy of all is a satisfied customer.

- Observation: Pay attention to your customer's actions and the things that make him or her happy when you are delivering service.

Keep in mind that in the context of client relations, the small interpersonal gestures mentioned above mean a great deal. They may alter how customers perceive you, which could ultimately harm your efforts to build goodwill with them.

CUSTOMER NEEDS

A customer is motivated to buy a product or service by a need they have. The most important factor determining which solution the customer chooses is the need, which can be known (i.e., the customer can express it in words) or unknown.

The most effective business strategy of all is a satisfied customer.

Utilizing the perspective of "jobs to be done" is one efficient method for defining and analyzing customer needs. Different categories can be used to categorize customer wants. A customer might, for instance, require a solution that meets particular requirements for functionality, price, or reliability.

The three basic categories of client needs are functional, social, and emotional needs.

1. Functional needs.

The functional demands are the most important of the three primary customer needs categories. Customers often assess alternative solutions based on whether they would aid in the accomplishment of a specific goal. They probably choose the good or service that best meets their requirements in terms of functionality. Depending on the customer's purchasing criteria, functional needs can range widely or be extremely narrow.

The most effective business strategy of all is a satisfied customer.

2. Social needs.

When a person uses a good or service, their social needs are related to how they want to be seen by other people. Even though social needs are typically not a customer's top priority when making a purchase, they might nevertheless have an impact on their choice.

Social needs are frequently harder for a business to pinpoint and differ greatly from client to consumer. You might hunt for patterns among your clients by comprehending diverse social wants.

If the vast majority of your customers adhere to a specific need, you should consider how it can enhance your product development, sales, and marketing procedures.

3. Emotional needs.

Because they frequently come second to functional needs, emotional needs are comparable to social needs. Emotional needs are different from social needs in that emotional needs are how a customer wants to feel after utilizing a product.

Although identifying a customer's emotional requirements can be challenging, businesses that do so can utilize the information to improve their product pitch.

Your brand must never disregard the importance of the emotional needs of your customers.

The most effective business strategy of all is a satisfied customer.

Chapter 4

CUSTOMER LOYALTY.

Customer loyalty is a continuous emotional bond between you and your customers that shows in their willingness to interact with you and make repeat purchases from you as opposed to your competition.

When a customer has a good experience with you, loyalty develops naturally and helps to build trust.

Some of the outcomes of Customer loyalty include:
1. Value Creation: Customer loyalty portrays your brand with integrity, quality and in a highly esteemed way.
2. Customer Retention: It will keep your customers committed to purchasing your products or services.

The most effective business strategy of all is a satisfied customer.

3. Customer References: Consistent customers will refer new customers to your brand.

Consistently observe that your customers' feedback is always positive. Their feedback determines how they remain loyal to your brand. Customer loyalty gives your brand a competitive advantage over others.

TYPES OF LOYAL CUSTOMERS.

When it comes to customer loyalty, the customer stays committed to your brand for different reasons such as price, quality, experience, and memories and the bond you shared with them makes them stable and devoted to your brand. Although individuals have various reasons for loyalty, it's pretty simple to categorize them into six different types.

1. Happy Customer

These types of loyal customers like your products or services, they have never complained, and have possibly patronized you several times.

But your competitors can easily steal them: all it takes is a better offer, a discount, or the formation of a new relationship.

2. Price-loyal

These types of customers are with you only because of the low prices. If they can save money somewhere else, they will leave and if you offer the best price again, they will return. It's pretty easy to keep this type of customer, but at an enormous cost.

3. Loyalty program-loyal

These types of customers are not loyal to your company, brand, or what you sell. They are only loyal to your loyalty program, and in many cases, only because your loyalty reward offers the best deal.

4. Convenience-loyal

These customers are simply devoted to your brand because it is simple to get in touch with, locate, and make purchases from. Price doesn't matter to a consumer who is committed to convenience: convenience is what keeps them coming back.

The most effective business strategy of all is a satisfied customer.

5. Loyal to freebies

These types of customers are not drawn to your brand because of what you sell but because of the other things, you offer. For instance, free Wi-Fi or infant changing tables, or free samples. Customers who are loyal to your freebies may buy from you only occasionally and don't contribute heavily to your revenue stream.

6. Truly loyal

These types of loyal customers are your advocates. They patronize your brand repeatedly, talk about their great experiences with your brand, and send their friends and family to you.

HOW TO BUILD AND MAINTAIN CUSTOMER LOYALTY.

1. Keep your customers engaged.

You must interact with your customers consistently. In this manner, customers develop a relationship with your brand and continue to remember you.

The most effective business strategy of all is a satisfied customer.

You also need to think about the mode of communication that would be best for them. Is it email or social media? What platform would best suit them? Facebook? Instagram? Twitter?

You also need to customize your communication and make it personalized to your users. One way to personalize communication is to communicate with your customers based on the actions taken about your business. For instance, it could be an email that is sent when they sign up for your loyalty program.

Then another email when they move to tier two of the program, or when they refer a friend; This way, the customer stays engaged. An email from you when they are celebrating significant milestones like their birthdays will be highly appreciated also.

While automation makes things easier, and more productive while being cost-effective, you do not want to subject your customers to consistent automation from the email response that they receive; from Facebook messenger response to the robot who 'picks up their call'.

The most effective business strategy of all is a satisfied customer.

However, in some situations, automation may not apply, for example, in an e-commerce store, it helps to have a 'human element' when dealing with your customers. You could have a live chat button for instance, where customers get to interact with real members of staff.

The dos and don'ts in communication.

- For communication to be effective, both parties must be able to participate.
- Customers should be able to send messages as well, so it is never just the brand that is always communicating.
- Customers need a platform where they can engage with the brand, not just the bots, and interact with it.
- Customer complaints and compliments should be immediately addressed by brands, and communication should never come off as a sales pitch.

2. Provide top-notch goods.

The primary driver of brand loyalty is high-quality goods. Make sure your product is of a good caliber and provides the advantages it ought to. Customers must believe that you are providing them with the best goods you are capable of providing. Continuous innovation is one approach to guarantee the excellent quality of your products. Keep finding ways to improve, either by adding more functionality to them, or simply adding new payment systems that are more secure and convenient.

3. Build a community.

You need to create online communities on social media which bring your customers together. You can start interesting conversations and allow the customers to share their stories too. It is also a good idea to bring value to the community by introducing community leaders and industry experts to the community.

The most effective business strategy of all is a satisfied customer.

By doing this, customers can have their issues addressed quickly, even by people who may not be necessarily affiliated with your brand, thereby bringing a more credible point of view.

Another way that you can build a community is by getting involved in some work whether voluntary or involuntary that showcases your brand as one that 'cares'.

4. Study your customers consistently.

You cannot communicate efficiently with someone you do not understand. It is therefore essential for brands to invest time in studying their customers to understand their pains and joys. You can do this by asking your customers questions in the community you built for your brand.

5. Aspire to build trust.

Remaining true to your word is one strategy for gaining customer loyalty. If there is a problem or complaint, and you promise to look into it, you need to ensure that you do so. If you promise to respond to a customer email or inquiry via social media, then do so.

The most effective business strategy of all is a satisfied customer.

You should always be genuine and respectful when apologizing for mistakes and rectifying them as soon as possible. In addition, DO NOT PROMISE SOMETHING THAT YOU CAN NOT DELIVER.

If your brand or company promises to deliver something, your customers automatically expect you to keep that promise, so you must strive to meet and exceed your customers' expectations. Failure to do so might make you lose trust.

6. Reward Customer Loyalty.

Customers feel great when they are rewarded, so you need to reward customers who are loyal to your brand. This is where loyalty programs come in. Rewards can be discounts, redeemable cash, or even free trips, depending on your brand. Ensure that your loyalty programs have a feeling of suspense to keep the customers engaged. They should not be complex but should be easy to use. Some brands will even go the extra mile to give their customers simple gifts and treats during their birthdays.

The most effective business strategy of all is a satisfied customer.

7. Offer great customer service

Customer service is another reason why customers would stop purchasing from a brand. Customer service focuses on how the customer feels. If they were treated well, they will be more willing to make repeat purchases, and even refer others. If they do not have a great customer experience, they will tell their friends and family too.

8. Keep your team updated.

It can be extremely unpleasant for your customers to need assistance, and it can be much more annoying if some of your staff are ignorant of the most recent changes to your product, payment method, or loyalty scheme. The need for customer loyalty needs to be communicated, and staff members should be encouraged to participate fully.

In conclusion, a business should never take customer loyalty for granted. It is an important component of success.

The most effective business strategy of all is a satisfied customer.

Chapter 5

SALES OBJECTION.

Practically every customer you interact with has concerns about deals or reasons they are hesitant to buy your product; if they didn't have reservations about the price, value, relevance to their situation, or their capacity to buy, they would have already purchased it.

Objection handling is a fundamental component of selling, yet it frequently acts as a significant roadblock when you're trying to move prospects through the pipeline. You could try to persuade yourself to recognize the complaints and send a parting email right away. But if there's even a remote chance that you'll succeed, you want to learn how to locate and eliminate these fears.

The most effective business strategy of all is a satisfied customer.

At the point when objections emerge, it isn't an ideal opportunity to surrender — it's a chance to reemphasize your item's worth.

Here, you will learn all that you want to realize about complaint dealing, including ways of disproving normal objections.

What is an objection to a sale?

A clear sign that you need to handle more areas of the buying process than you previously thought is a sales objection, which is any concern a prospect has about a barrier preventing them from purchasing from you.

A sales objection typically stems from a buyer's "lack" of a particular capability. A prospect objects to a deal when they believe they lack the resources, motivation, need, or capacity to purchase from you at a certain moment. Despite being one of the most difficult and annoying components of sales, objections are not always fruitless.

The most effective business strategy of all is a satisfied customer.

What is Objection management?

A customer's perspective may be changed or their worries may be alleviated through the process of objection management.

If a prospect express concerns about the good or service a salesperson is offering, objection management occurs when the salesperson reacts in a way that allays the concern and permits the deal to proceed. The most common objections focus on the cost, product fit, or rivals. An objection may occasionally be handled with a straightforward dismissal.

Some salespeople quarrel with their customers or use threats to make them give in, but this isn't real objection handling. In those situations, prospects frequently become even more convinced of their viewpoint than before, and those salespeople usually end up damaging the relationship and trust they had built with the customers.

Instead of informing your potential customer that they are mistaken, assist them in independently reaching a different conclusion. And if you are unable to convince them, they are likely a poor fit.

Making the distinction between sales objections and brush-offs is also crucial.

Objections are real, but brush-offs are just justifications. A brush-off is equivalent to saying, "I don't want to talk to you," but an objection could be described as, "I see the value in your product, but I'm not sure about buying it for X reason". Objections should be taken more seriously than brush-offs.

Dealing with objections.

Dealing with objections is a common yet very frustrating aspect of selling. Every salesperson needs to be proficient in a few certain actions and abilities to carry out the procedure. These include being aware of your surroundings, learning about your subject, demonstrating empathy, and asking meaningful, open-ended questions.

The most effective business strategy of all is a satisfied customer.

HOW TO DEAL WITH OBJECTIONS.

1. Be aware of your surroundings

There is no universal or magic method for answering objections that can address any issue a potential customer might have. You must have a firm understanding of your current sales situation, the type of deal you're chasing, and your prospect's demands and interests, among other things.

To properly address a prospect's objections, it is essential to comprehend the situations that are influencing them. As your interactions with prospects develop, you must continue to be situationally aware.

2. Promoting Empathy

Sales objections are a common occurrence, and many, if not most of the time, are valid issues. You must therefore resist getting furious with your prospects when they push back a little. Every sales effort depends on empathy.

The most effective business strategy of all is a satisfied customer.

Selling to a prospect should not be done solely for financial gain; rather, it should be done because your product or service is best suited to meet their needs. As a result, you must always consider their wants and interests. If you remain conscious of their problems and circumstances and approach them with empathy and compassion, you may be in a position to anticipate the objections they might make and effectively answer them.

3. Ask Open-ended, thoughtful questions.

Every other argument made here can be furthered by having the ability to pose meaningful, open-ended questions. If you want to comprehend and successfully address the objections raised by your prospects, you must first identify and address their primary concerns.

A good place to start is by posing pertinent, diplomatic questions and allowing ample time for them to respond. Avoid asking inquiries that can only be answered with a simple "yes" or "no" and don't be afraid to take advantage of quiet.

Allow your customers to express their opinions. Feel out their worries and position yourself to anticipate any objections they may have.

Importance of dealing with objections.

The worst thing you can do for a deal is to put off addressing sales concerns until the very end. The longer the buyer has an opinion, the stronger it is likely to be and the more difficult it will be to change it.

1. An engaged buyer will frequently raise objections.

The customer's objections will grow more precise and represent their thoughts as the sale progresses. You have the chance to adapt, adjust, and overcome if there is a situational ambiguity on their part. Even at the very end, when the cost is frequently a concern, you have the chance to profit from the customer's full engagement.

The most effective business strategy of all is a satisfied customer.

2. You can take advantage of the chance to provide value.
A sales conversation that is more in-depth and fruitful often results from an objection. After all, customers are genuinely seeking clarification on their questions so seize the opportunity and offer new facts or information that add value after getting a sense of where they are going.

3. They can help you qualify or disqualify a buyer.
To avoid wasting time throwing objections back and forth with potential customers who will never write a check, objections are a smart approach to qualify prospects. If the ratio for qualified leads falls below 50%, you'd likely be better off more aggressively disqualifying prospects. You'll need to replace those disqualified prospects with a regular supply of new ones, but you will at least have time.

Start making use of these important advantages, and you'll not only be able to handle objections better but also see how effective they can be in advancing your brand's goals.

The most effective business strategy of all is a satisfied customer.

TYPES OF OBJECTIONS TO SALES.

Most sales objections are based on some sort of "lack," and they often originate from a valid point of view. When a customer objects, they frequently mention that they are unable to purchase at this time.

If you know what you're doing, you can typically find ways to get around those "lacks," which are frequently misplaced. Let's examine some of the most typical objections in sales in more detail.

1. Insufficient Need

To sell something, a customer must require it. Sometimes, there may be nothing you can do to assist the prospect. However, you are to blame if the potential customer appears to be a good fit but doesn't perceive the value in what you have to offer. You're either not connecting, not considering all the needs, or not addressing the proper need.

When examining needs, keep the following in mind:

a) Concentrate on results instead of method.

Results are what people buy, not processes. You distinguish yourself by concentrating on the value you provide and the results you'll produce rather than the specifics of how you'll do it.

b) Become knowledgeable about the customer's company, sector, and rivals.

Knowing this can assist you in identifying areas where you can bring value and how your services might be beneficial. You can learn a lot about their competitors' strategies and tactics by doing this.

2. Absence of Urgency

Money is not a concern, the customer trusts you, and you have established a relationship. The customer, however, is unable to advance the project because they are overloaded and waiting for the "perfect time". When this occurs, you haven't adequately shown how your answer would affect things.

By concentrating on these two forms of consequences, you can aid the customer in appreciating how you can assist them:

a) Impact with logic.

The main focus of the rational impact is on calculating the ROI (Return on Investment) and developing the business case for continuity. If your needs analysis was done successfully, you should be able to provide statistics that show how your solution has affected society. The customer must recognize a definite monetary worth. Lack of ROI results in a lack of urgency.

b) The emotional influence.

A solution's emotional influence is just as significant as its numerical value. Consider the customer's goals to identify their emotional motivators.

Aspirations focus on the things the buyer wants to alter as well as the possible rewards associated with them, going beyond the pain and those things the customer must change.

The most effective business strategy of all is a satisfied customer.

Focus on the following important questions to paint this aspirational picture: What would happen to your financial status if you were able to do this? What repercussions might you experience if you wait?

3. A Lack of Faith

Trust is determined by whether the customer is confident in your ability to keep your commitments. If they do, you will have taken a step further toward the transaction, and the risk will be lower. This trust needs to be earned the traditional way. This is how:

a) Conduct research first.

The more familiar you are with the customer's business and industry, the more assured they will be in your abilities.

b) Be sincere and demonstrate interest.

Be at ease, smile, and think positively. Inquire about your potential customer's personal life in addition to their life as potential business partners. People easily trust whom they like.

The most effective business strategy of all is a satisfied customer.

c) Keep advocacy and research in check.

Find the right number of questions and promotion of your services. Telling stories is one of the best ways to advocate. The greatest method to establish credibility is by providing pertinent examples and tales that demonstrate how you have benefited organizations with similar needs. Make sure to clearly state the outcomes and results when using stories to illustrate intangible concepts.

4. Lack of Funds

The cost objection is typical. By following these recommendations, you may, however, get past almost any pricing objection, receive your full rates, and prevent discounting.

a) Pay close attention and confirm whether money is the issue.

When your prospect expresses concern about money, pay close attention to the objection and confirm that it relates to money.

Price complaints frequently cover up underlying, non-financial problems.

Asking questions such as, "If money were no object, what would be your ideal solution?" will help you identify the true objection. It will be simpler to resolve financial concerns if you and the prospect can arrive at a shared vision.

b) Steer clear of discussing the expense structure. Frequently, a potential client will request that you break down the pricing into billable hours so they can better understand it. Avoid discussing cost structures since doing so will lead to you defending your price rather than your value.

c) Limit the scope to cut costs. Never reduce your price without also changing the deliverables. Arbitrariness breeds mistrust. Ask what portion of your solution you don't want after going over each component. This results in either a scope reduction or the prospect realizing the entire package are the best option.

You can identify the actual problems earlier if you are aware of the typical sorts of sales objections.

The most effective business strategy of all is a satisfied customer.

This will enable you to swiftly implement a plan to recognize, address, explore, and eventually overcome sales objections, enabling you to complete deals more quickly. An objection is not a rejection; it is merely a request for further information. Make sure you are speaking and listening rather than rushing to a conclusion.

EFFECTIVE TACTICS FOR GETTING PAST OBJECTIONS.

1. Use active listening techniques.

First and foremost, make sure you are employing active listening techniques to comprehend what your prospect is saying when they express their issues to you. As your prospect explains their concerns, listen to understand rather than to comment. Give them time to finish their sentences without being interrupted, and allow them the freedom to express any reservations or objections.

The most effective business strategy of all is a satisfied customer.

2. Recite what you heard back.

Repeat what you heard after your prospect has presented their objections to make sure you comprehend them. This will not only help you understand their ideas better, but it will also make your prospect feel heard and respected, both of which are crucial for developing trust.

3. Verify your prospect's worries.

Continue establishing trust with your prospect by empathizing with them and confirming their perspective once you've demonstrated that you know where they're coming from. But that doesn't imply that you must undervalue your product or endorse a rival.

4. Pose follow-up inquiries.

When objections are mentioned, you want to make every effort to keep the dialogue flowing naturally. Asking follow-up questions might be a skillful technique to keep your prospect talking if you notice their retraction.

The most effective business strategy of all is a satisfied customer.

Make sure to use open-ended questions that allow your prospect to continue discussing your product instead of queries that can be replied to with a simple "yes" or "no." The more details they provide you, the more you have to work with to maybe close the deal.

5. Make use of social proof.
Sharing the experience of another customer who had similar worries and later experienced success with your product may be a successful strategy, depending on the nature of your prospect's worry.

6. Determine a definite day and time for the follow-up.
Give your potential customer the space and time they need to consider their alternatives if they ask for more time to do so. You don't want to abandon them, though. So that too much time doesn't pass, schedule a definite time and day for a follow-up and offer to address any questions they may have while they think things over.

The most effective business strategy of all is a satisfied customer.

7. Be prepared for sales resistance.

Ultimately, anticipating sales objections is the best course of action for dealing with them. You're much less likely to be off your game when you're ready for objections to arise.

When prospects resist, having a set of impartial ideas to provide them might help keep the sale moving. They're usually open to hearing you out if you have a solution to provide because you took the time to listen to the customers and consider their viewpoints instead of responding in kind. It's also beneficial to keep track of the objections you encounter most frequently. When you are aware of what to anticipate, you can spend more time mastering your responses.

Sales representatives should perform role-plays to improve their ability to handle objections. Exchange common complaints, responses, and constructive criticism with other sales representatives in your team.

In conclusion, instead of avoiding objections, embrace them.

The most effective business strategy of all is a satisfied customer.

Chapter 6

CUSTOMER RETENTION

This is a method or attitude used by a business to ensure that customers continually request their services, as well as an action to acquire, keep, and watch over customers over time to prevent customer loss to a rival.

The ability of a business to keep customers making repeated purchases and prevent them from switching to the competition is known as customer retention. It serves as a performance gauge that shows whether or not they are satisfied with the caliber of your service and product. It's a method to keep your customers on your side and to keep them safe and secure. You may develop a better strategy to attract and keep loyal customers s by being aware of the many types of loyal customers and the people you value.

The most effective business strategy of all is a satisfied customer.

Your top objective should always be retaining customers. An increase in brand-loyal clients boosts sales and increases revenue for your business. Therefore, it is advantageous to keep your devoted customers.

BENEFITS OF CUSTOMER RETENTION.

1. Cost-effectiveness

Getting new clients is more expensive than keeping the ones you already have. According to various customer service statistics, it can cost between three and thirty times as much to acquire a new customer as it does to keep an existing one. It can be difficult to persuade a potential new customer of the value that your product or service can provide them, so even if you do acquire new clients, it may take some time before you see a return on your investment.

When you have repeat customers, you may concentrate less on developing new marketing plans and more on enhancing customer satisfaction with your company's products and services.

The most effective business strategy of all is a satisfied customer.

New customers need a lot of support before they can understand your business operations, in addition to the costs associated with the acquisition. Customers who he strong brand loyalty are already familiar with your operational procedures. As a result, they won't require as much support, which ultimately turns out to be more affordable than the support expenditures associated with new systems. customers. This is one of the explanations for why many companies claim that their current clients are the best.

2. extremely tolerant and supportive.

In business, things don't always go as planned. Technical issues or simple errors happen occasionally. Customers who are loyal to your brand will be more understanding in these situations and give you more time to address the issue. If other clients start to complain, they can start to bolster your brand. Similar to how devoted customers will be understanding and forthcoming if the bugs are brought on by a product you are launching and testing.

The most effective business strategy of all is a satisfied customer.

3. immunity from the opposition

You can be less concerned about competition if you have customers who are loyal to your brand. This is because your devoted clients currently adore what you are providing, particularly if you continue to make changes. You can concentrate on ways to reverse-engineer your competitors' practices and apply them to your advantage rather than having to adopt tactics like price reduction to keep clients.

4. Repeated transactions and purchases.

Customers who are devoted to your brand pay more. They will adhere to your promotions, and offers, and even make an effort to get the best deals possible. Your chances of making money are higher if you can retain customers or get them to buy from you repeatedly.

5. Sincere criticism

You may use timely and honest feedback from loyal customers to enhance both the quality of your goods and services and the experience that customers have when using them.

The most effective business strategy of all is a satisfied customer.

Potentially dishonest reviews may not come from new clients. The majority of the time, they will offer no input at all. Most of the time, they will sample your product and try another if they don't like even a little component of it.

6. A good source for referrals.
Loyal customers are more likely to be joyful, and joyful people will tell other people about their wonderful experiences. These customers are excellent for boosting word-of-mouth and are more likely to support the company meaning they might tell others about their experiences.

The Dos and Don'ts for customer service representatives.

Some words are off-limits when providing customer support. You are not permitted to use certain words when speaking to customers. As a customer service agent, you will come into circumstances where your words can make or break a customer engagement.

The following words and phrases should never be used since they aggravate and frustrate customers:

- No
- I'm not sure
- That's not my department/not that's my job
- You're correct, that's not good.
- Relax
- I'm currently busy
- Call me back, please
- I'm not to blame
- You need to speak with my boss
- By when do you want it?

1. No: Refusing a customer's request is a sign of disdain for them. The customer feels discouraged, and it could even start an unneeded argument. Though you might have to refuse something, instead of declining, try to find another method to handle the situation.

The most effective business strategy of all is a satisfied customer.

2. I'm not sure: Never give the customer the appearance that you don't know the answer to their question or inquiry. When you say "I don't know" to a customer, they will get the notion that you don't feel like providing them with the information they require. Saying "I'll find out" or "Let me look into this and get back to you as soon as possible" will be preferable.

3. That's not my job/not that's my department: Always kindly send your customer to the right department or authority that will handle the issue at hand. When you are requested to perform a task for which you are not qualified or have the authority, it is preferable to say, "Let me transfer you to the person who can help you right away" rather than saying, "That's not my job/department".

4. You're right, that's not good: It seems like you could just as easily correct the customer. The phrase "you are right" is poor customer service.

The most effective business strategy of all is a satisfied customer.

Many unskilled customer service professionals believe that by empathizing with the customer's situation, they may win the customer over rather than take action to address the issue. If a customer displays irritation or displeasure, do not add to their distress by empathizing. While attempting to remedy the issue, show empathy for the customer. It helps to use appropriate language, such as, "I understand your irritation, let's see how we can fix this situation."

5. Relax: Give disgruntled or irate customers s a chance to vent (within reason), and they will eventually find some peace. Telling them to "calm down" is disrespectful and frequently just serves to enrage them even more. One of the best phrases for customer service is "I'm sorry"; it calms even the angriest of customers and enables you to start working on a customer's issue or request and "meet him/her halfway."

The most effective business strategy of all is a satisfied customer.

Although you don't have to agree with the customer to apologize, it is a way to show empathy and get past the immediate, unpleasant emotions.

6. I'm busy right now: This statement devalues a customer and may cause them to leave. When another customer phones or comes to your service area, you are frequently assisting the first one. To throw off a customer and say you are too busy to help them is completely different from gently asking them to wait or asking them to be patient. One of the cardinal sins of customer service is leaving customers waiting or on hold.

Being "too busy" is the same as telling someone you don't care or that they are not significant. Make sure the customer knows you value their business and are aware of their presence. Saying "I'll be with you in a moment" or "Please hold, and I'll be right there" is preferable.

The most effective business strategy of all is a satisfied customer.

7. Call me back: This request demonstrates a lack of concern on the part of the customer service agent for the needs and desires of the customer. Always give the customer a call because you value their patronage and are attentive to their needs. Good customer service includes being proactive.

8. That's not my fault: You are still a member of the team as long as you play a crucial role in the department where the problem of the customer arose from the business. The instinctive response is to defend oneself if an angry customer accuses you of causing an issue, whether the accusation is true or false.

This is not, however, the optimal course of action. The customer's issue has to be resolved. You can address the issue more quickly, with less stress and tension, by putting off the urge to defend yourself and concentrating instead on the needs of the customer. It is preferable to say "Let's investigate our options for solving this issue".

The most effective business strategy of all is a satisfied customer.

9. You Need to Speak with My Supervisor: If your customer doesn't insist on speaking with the supervisor, why would they want to speak with him or her? Never press your customer into talking to your manager. Always try to find a solution to the issue, or you can ask your supervisor for assistance. It is preferable to reply, "Let me find out for you."

10. By when do you want it? Customers frequently have unreasonable expectations, particularly when it comes to timing. Your initial emotion can be irritation, and you might want to say something rude. The best course of action, nevertheless, is to refrain from being unfavorable and leaving a bad impression. It would be better to reply, "I'll call you back as soon as I find out".

Some other phrases to avoid include:
- "I apologize for that"
- "You have a choice"
- "I don't get to decide that"
- "I can't," but it can be done."

The most effective business strategy of all is a satisfied customer.

We can term this a customer service initiative because it brings a fine line between ordinary customer service and extraordinary customer service. There are some customer services you can provide to a person and you win that person for life.

This entails exerting more effort than you would ordinarily put forth in providing customer service, usually to exceed customers' expectations so they will remember the interaction.

The customer service person and sometimes even a business or organization looking to provide a certain service are responsible for demonstrating a customer service initiative, that is what will make the customer return to the same location at all times for support.

One thought that should cross your mind as a customer service representative is: "What will the customer think of me when we've had a one-on-one conversation?".

The most effective business strategy of all is a satisfied customer.

Being proactive might occasionally help you outperform your rivals since you want to take extra steps that they are not taking.

The program makes the difference between providing customers with basic service and providing them with the best service that wins you a lifelong customer.

Why should a customer choose your business over another? If a customer sees the quality of your products and services, they will stay with you.

Who doesn't appreciate wonderful things? If another customer is enjoying a service, he or she will take advantage of it.

These "goodwill efforts" go above and beyond the call of duty, leaving the customers ecstatic and remembering the transaction or occasion.

THEY HELP YOUR CUSTOMERS CREATE GOOD MEMORIES.

The most effective business strategy of all is a satisfied customer.

However, "poor initiatives" restrict your ability to manage customer relationships and work against you and your business.

THEY LEAVE YOUR CUSTOMER WITH DESPAIRING MEMORY

The most effective business strategy of all is a satisfied customer.

Chapter 7

COMMUNICATION AND RAPPORT.

Creating intimacy between your brand and your customers to deepen your relationship and communication with them is the process of building rapport. You must learn to sympathize with your clients, take a real interest in them, and establish a mutual link of trust to build rapport with them, especially over the phone. Making customers feel valued and taken into consideration is crucial to delivering excellent service and boosting sales.

One of the most crucial qualities of a customer service professional is the ability to establish rapport with the individuals they are there to assist.

Advantages of developing a rapport with your customers
- It builds trust
- It boosts customer loyalty
- it aids in pardon

The most effective business strategy of all is a satisfied customer.

Features of rapport-building include:

1. For rapport to be effective, it must be genuine.

2. If rapport is fake, it doesn't work well.

3. It helps you get to know your clientele better.

How to establish a rapport

1. Make first contact

2. Make friendly greetings.

3. Use client names, such as Ms. Jane.

4. Be enthusiastic

5. Give the customer your name.

6. Customize your customer service

7. Pay attention to just one customer at a time, use the statement "You have my full focus right now.

8. Use a word of appreciation

9. A follow-up

The most effective business strategy of all is a satisfied customer.

Taking steps to establish rapport.

1. Talk about their hobbies and interests.

People want to talk about themselves and this makes them a friend, so I try to pick up on their interests, whether they are cooking, painting, camping, etc. This is a terrific method because people feel comfortable talking about themselves. When you demonstrate a sincere interest in something they care about, it helps people feel at ease and increases your likeability.

2. Enquire regarding their projects

"Starting a conversation with what your customers are making always works". This makes the customers feel that you care about them, and you discover useful information about the customers you serve and making it easier to encourage customers to talk about themselves.

The most effective business strategy of all is a satisfied customer.

It could help establish rapport because people like to talk about themselves or what they're working on, and second, it could help you better understand the needs of the customer.

3. Describe a personal characteristic.

To encourage customers to open up about themselves, by introducing yourself and telling the customer a bit about yourself.

4. Say happy birthday to them.

"You can wish a customer a happy late or early birthday if their birthday is less than two weeks away from the present date."

Customers are typically pleased when you remember their birthday.

You'll be able to utilize this approach quite frequently without overusing it if you send it two weeks before the actual date.

The most effective business strategy of all is a satisfied customer.

5. Request feedback from your customers.

Asking customers for guidance might make them feel at ease and naturally inclined to want to assist you because people like to be experts.

6. Compliment your customer.

Some people can be worried about the fine line between complimenting someone and acting inappropriately and flirtatiously.

For instance, if you are familiar with the brand or genuinely like the style of a customer's watch, you might comment. Request their name.

You can respectfully ask a question if the name is unusual or unusual-sounding: When you say, "That's an unusual name—I'm curious where it came from or what it means," you almost always receive a fascinating explanation for the name and the person opens up."

How to establish a rapport with irate customers.

1. Let Them Exhale: Allow your customers to express their feelings to you if they are upset or angry.

2. Recognize what they are saying as if you were in their position.

3. Apologize.

4. help yourself.

5. Offer a resolution.

6. fulfill all of their needs.

5. Follow up repeatedly.

Maintaining partnerships between brands and customers requires excellent rapport. Once people stick with your brand for a while. They'll join the family of your brand.

The most effective business strategy of all is a satisfied customer.

Establishing rapport in a live conversation.

You must establish rapport in your chat interactions.

1. In private conversations, use personal pronouns like "I" or "I have reverted your account, kindly check through."

2. Use the word "We" to represent your company, as in Your response has been received, and your order is on its way.

3. Recognize the worries of your customers

A sincere reaction and a kind parting from you will persuade the customer to keep using your product.

Chapter 8

THE PROCESS OF CLOSURE.

This process entails walking your customer through each solution you are presenting. When you inform them of every step of your services, it demonstrates that you are engaged in resolving their problems at that particular time.

Giving your customers quick updates and successfully wrapping up your interactions with them are part of the closing process.

The following stages are involved:

1. Explain what will come next, such as "Okay, I'll review your work, or I'll be with you, but I just checked your profile, and it shows you haven't been active in days."

The most effective business strategy of all is a satisfied customer.

2. Finish on a positive note with a fond farewell, such as, "Thank you so much for calling today."

3. Hold out on hanging up or leaving until your customer has responded.

4. Make your conclusion compelling enough for people to stay.

TELEPHONE ETIQUETTE.

Telephone conversation is not what you say but how you say it.

When you pick up the phone, your voice tone takes precedence over your body language and visual cues. The majority of the message you convey to the customer over the phone comes from voice inflection and attitude.

For instance:

- A flat voice tone is perceived by the customer as, "I don't like my job and would rather be somewhere else"

- A Slow-pitch and presentation are perceived as, "Do not bother me, I am depressed and lonely."

- A fast, high-pitched voice conveys the message "I am excited and ecstatic!"
- A loud voice is perceived as "I'm angry and violent".

A customer's opinion of you is very important.

EXECELLENT TELEPHONE ETIQUETTE

Contrary to more nuanced body language, telephone etiquette is universal and unaffected by culture. The telephone is frequently a customer's first or last point of contact with a business or organization. One of the least expensive and most cost-effective ways to provide better customer service is to be telephone friendly.

Picking up the phone.

The way a business answers the phone can reveal a lot about how they handle both customers and staff.

A positive tone and the proper words spoken in the proper order leave a good first impression and begin the brand-customer relationships on the right foot.

Steps for answering a call.

1. Within three rings, pick up the phone. Multiple rings indicate chaos in your office or the carelessness of your business or organization.

2. Welcome the caller by saying "hi" or "good morning." Good manners demonstrate respect to the caller.

3. Identify yourself by saying "Hello, my name is Charles". This is a courtesy that allows the customer to hold you responsible for the quality of your service and helps to customize the customer service experience. He or she now has a reference point and a person to call when they make a follow-up call.

You are anticipating that the person will explain why he or she wants to speak with you. This will aid in separating customers from merely passing acquaintances.

The greeting is crucial because it establishes the mood and manner of the entire exchange. This welcome algorithm can even be used to turn infrequent contacts into paying customers.

Depending on the business, the opening statement could be recorded to keep the same tone as you serve additional clients. If that is not the case, you must make sure that you are speaking in a loud voice while introducing yourself to the customer, regardless of how exhausted you are. After all, the customer is unaware of your working conditions and believes that you are being paid for the work you are doing.

STRESS MANAGEMENT.

A competent customer service professional must possess the ability to manage their stress. Typically, customer service representatives experience burnout from two sources:

- Regular demands that are repeated
- Frustrated customers.

If representatives don't control their reactions, the combination could result in tension. Here are some stress-relieving suggestions to help you remain composed and maintain perspective.

1. Avoid soaking up the annoyance of your customers. Don't take it personally; their frustration has nothing to do with you. All they can think about in their emotional state is how upset they are. Most people are unaware of the effect they may be having on you. Any exaggerations and personal assaults should be ignored. They could not be thinking right now. Sometimes even mild exaggerations cause stress reactions. Never let it affect you negatively.

2. Keep in mind that a perturbed customer is a pleasant person who has momentarily taken on the appearance of a wolf. Consider them to be generally sensible and in a positive or neutral attitude. They most likely called you before with a standard question and everything was OK. You're currently causing a behavioral radar blip for them. Remember that somewhere among them is a lovely person, and if you maintain your composure and cooperate with them, you'll find that nice client once more. If you keep hoping they'll change, they usually will apologize and thank you gratefully.

3. When customers are dissatisfied, their actions are a response to unfulfilled expectations. Finding out what they expect will help you calm down, maintain your composure, and keep the dialogue on issue-solving. Continue concentrating on what you can do to bridge the gap between their unmet expectations and their experience with the services and goods offered by your business. Customers are more receptive to alternative solutions when they are treated with respect and professionalism.

The most effective business strategy of all is a satisfied customer.

4. Make a deal with yourself before your shift begins that you'll maintain control of the calls and your emotions. The customer responds when you're in charge, and the dialogue is shorter and less intense. Their annoyance "pushes our buttons," which makes us less productive. Instead of having a conversational tone, the call is emotional. If you find yourself "falling off the wagon," take a moment to collect yourself, then vow to stay in control for the remainder of your shift. Even though the absence of tension you'll experience at the end of your shift will be reward enough, find a method to treat yourself for your first day "in control."

5. Maintain a good work/life balance. One of my favorite call center representatives keeps perspective by placing a recent family photo in his cube at eye level. It depicts the most recent family vacation. He uses the picture as a reminder that serving customers is his work and that his family is his life when calls get difficult. What values do you hold most dear in your daily life? As a reminder to keep perspective, bring a piece of your hobbies to work.

The most effective business strategy of all is a satisfied customer.

6. Log your laughs. Keep a list of words that will help you recall the situation. After a call, if you're feeling anxious and down, have a peek at a funny entry to help you feel better. When you're not at work, keep an eye out for amusing stories in books, movies, or real life to add to your laugh journal. It might be therapeutic to laugh with coworkers about trying phone calls, but it's better not to dwell on bad situations for too long. Consult your laugh journal and practice good humor!

7. Keep in mind that stress has a physical effect. Eat for reduced stress and mental clarity. Consider designating a no-sugar zone in your office. Even though stress can make you reach for sugar, the feel-good "rush" will pass after 30 minutes. You may be more sensitive to emotional responses when you have the sugar blues. Many people discover that increasing their protein intake keeps them optimistic.

Check out high-protein snacks like nuts, seeds, and sunflower seeds to see if there is a difference. It's crucial to consume plenty of water.

The most effective business strategy of all is a satisfied customer.

Dehydration or a lack of protein can cause a foggy and frustrated feeling. You'll feel more at ease and in control throughout the day if you eat for success.

Chapter 9

TROUBLESHOOTING AND ESCALATION.

This entails looking for any anomalies that might have an impact on the customer experience. Applications are used by every business to address customer complaints. The employee must check the available applications while posing pertinent questions to perform troubleshooting efficiently.

On the first call, troubleshooting aims to address customer complaints. Some problems, however, cannot be treated on the spot; instead, they are forwarded to certain pertinent units or teams, commonly referred to as the back-end units. This is where Escalation comes in.

The most effective business strategy of all is a satisfied customer.

Customer service representatives must first do their part by conducting thorough research, using all available resources, and asking pertinent questions before they can escalate a problem.

A customer service representative must note the following if they are about to escalate a problem as the process may aggravate a customer:

1. Place a customer on hold.
When the customers say "yes" or "no," ask them if you can put them on hold, and ensure you clarify that it will only last a short while.
Customers should be informed of the reason you have them on hold. And thank the customers who held.

2. Making a call transfer.
Ask the customer if they mind being transferred; listen for a "yes" or "no" response; and describe the transfer's purpose and recipient.

3. Message taking.

Positively describe your coworker's absence without going into too much detail. Describe the meeting, conference, briefing, or training that your coworker is attending. Do not refer to someone as ill, too drunk to report to work, never called in today, unable to be located, that you are unsure of their whereabouts, or that they "were just here".

Indicate a timeframe that is reasonable for the coworker's return. Give the caller a hand, take a transfer to another employee, or message. If a coworker is on vacation and won't be back, It is OK to claim that someone is on vacation and they won't be in the office for a while but skip specifics.

While such details may appear benign and even hilarious, they provide the wrong impression to individuals seeking care.

4. Call is terminated.

The best telephone etiquette ends with this. A good customer care person will wrap up the call by reiterating any activities that have been agreed upon as well as what will be done to assist or serve the customer.

5. Quickly reply to your business email.

All businesses should place a high priority on promptly responding to business emails. In addition, Email is a vital channel for communication with your customer, and they frequently use it to determine your level of credibility.

Consider a company that requires more than five days to respond to a straightforward query. The Internet—seemed to have existed forever. If a customer must wait that long for a response, they will probably do business elsewhere.

When sending business emails, response time is no longer than 24 hours. Without exceptions, you are faring better than many other businesses at that rate.

Consider responding to your business email twice per day, separated by 12 hours, if you want your customer service to stand out. It is sometimes advisable to email your direct competitors and pose as a prospect to check out their offer. Send them multiple times over a period of days. Check out the weekends, Mondays, and Fridays in particular. Keep track of how long it takes them to respond and put a plan in place to outperform them in the game of business email.

CREATING A GOOD FIRST IMPACT.

Every salesperson in every industry understands the value of establishing a good first impression. Salespeople are aware that how their potential client perceives them in the first 30 seconds of engagement will determine their success and ability to support themselves. Effective salesmen establish a rapport with potential customers almost immediately. Customers favor them,
then purchase their offering after taking their recommendations.

The most effective business strategy of all is a satisfied customer.

The truth is that we favor doing business with people we respect and like. Building a customer's trust and confidence depends on first impressions. According to a proverb, "You will never have a second chance to make a first impression".

Here are some strategies for making a favorable impression, some of which have already been discussed:

- Consideration of the demands of the customer
- Generosity
- Appear presentable
- Sincere smile
- Individual accountability for a customer
- Rapid resolution of customer issues
- Providing right-away assistance
- A friendly vocal tone
- Referring to the customer by name in a dialogue
- Courteous and polite behavior

The most effective business strategy of all is a satisfied customer.

The following are some elements that provide a bad impression:
- Keeping the customer waiting
- Not immediately returning calls
- Failing to say "please" or "thank you"
- Speaking rudely or loudly to customers or coworkers
- Appearing messy or unconcerned with your appearance
- A shaky handshake
- Making an ironic remark
- A lack of morality
- Not smiling, making expressions, frowning, and behaving distant
- Addressing or providing service to a customer while concentrating on another work.

Don't forget that impressions stick with the people you encounter, especially customers, and once registered, negative impressions are challenging to shake off.

The most effective business strategy of all is a satisfied customer.

Remember that once formed, negative impressions are challenging to shake, especially once they have been registered with customers.

CUSTOMER SATISFACTION

Customer satisfaction evaluates how well or poorly your product, service, and entire experience live up to or beyond customer expectations. Simply said, it entails attending to all of your customer's demands whenever they arise, both now and in the future.

In essence, you will succeed or fail based on how satisfied they are with your brand, your product, your service, your messaging, and more.

Customer loyalty is the best way to survive in this fiercely competitive business market since it leads to customer happiness. Every brand wants as many customers as possible since they are a valuable asset. The likelihood that your customers will remain loyal to your brand increases with their level of satisfaction.

The most effective business strategy of all is a satisfied customer.

Therefore, it's crucial to continuously measure customer satisfaction.

The simple formula for calculating customer satisfaction.

1. Create plans and goals.
2. Survey your customers.
3. Select the timeframe or the triggers and timing.
4. Review the data.
5. Make the necessary changes.
6. Develop Results.

Techniques for measuring customer satisfaction through surveys.

There are a variety of techniques, however, in the rapidly evolving world of technology, these new techniques are simple to understand, and use:

1. Consider Net Promoter Score (NPS).
2. Transcripts of live chats
3. Mentions on social media
4. Promotional emails
5. Brief Message Service (SMS)
6. Churn Rate
7. Follow-up polls

1. Net Promoter Score (NPS)

Popular customer satisfaction surveys like NPS are used to collect both quantitative and qualitative information about customers. If you wish to use this type of survey with the advice offered in the following part, you'll need to adopt some kind of customer feedback software.

Net Promoter Scores are used to measure customer satisfaction and forecast company expansion. The corporate world was changed by this validated metric. Based on the question asked, the survey measures the perceptions of your customers.

Your client will provide rates in response to the query. Depending on their response, customers fall into one of three categories: 0 (not at all likely), 10 (very likely).

An NPS is calculated using 3 categories.
You will use the response to the following key question to determine your NPS on a scale of 0 to 10:
How likely are you to suggest [brand] to a friend or coworker?

The following are the groups of respondents:
1. Promoters (scoring 9–10) are devoted aficionados who will continue to purchase and recommend products thereby promoting growth.
2. Passives (scores of 7-8) are contented but unenthusiastic customers who are open to competing products.
3. Detractors (scoring 0-6) are dissatisfied customers who can harm your brand and obstruct your progress brought on by unfavorable word of mouth.

The Net Promoter Score can range from a low of -100 (if every customer is a Detractor) to a high of 100 by calculating the proportion of Detractors from the percentage of Promoters (if every customer is a Promoter).

2. Transcripts of live chats.

The advantages of live chat transcripts are comparable to those of surveys or Net Promoter Scores. However, it's not necessary to solicit participation from customers; simply review prior chats
captured by your live chat program. Customers frequently provide a wealth of both direct and indirect feedback during these talks, and this data is useful for assessing customer satisfaction.

And that goes beyond just product-specific criticism. You may find out if customers are pleased with your company's website, customer support, and sales staff by encouraging salespeople to solicit feedback immediately within the chat.

The most effective business strategy of all is a satisfied customer.

3. Social Media

Comments on social media show how customers feel about the marketing materials for your company. Your followers have an immediate avenue to learn about any new campaigns you launch to publish user comments. These remarks are special because they concentrate on your messaging, which is challenging to discuss in a follow-up survey or live chat transcript.

Social media can also be used as a means of gathering customer feedback. You can use a poll you publish on Twitter or Instagram to track customer satisfaction. This channel has the advantage of being free to use and providing you with direct access to your customer.

4. Promotional emails.

Email is a great platform for interaction and gathering feedback. You may easily include a link to one of your surveys in a weekly newsletter because the people who subscribe to it have shown a clear interest in your company. Alternatively, you might include the survey right in the email.

The most effective business strategy of all is a satisfied customer.

5. Brief Message Service (SMS).

Texting, or SMS, is another effective method for getting feedback. Sending messages in bulk is reasonably inexpensive, and it enables you to place a survey in your customers' hands.

Additionally, if you want a free option, you can utilize a well-known chat software such as Twitter or WhatsApp.

6. Churn Rate.

There will always be a certain proportion of your customer that won't provide you with a review or any feedback. So, how do you include these customers in your analysis of customer satisfaction? Look at your customer churn rate. This is the proportion of customers who discontinue doing business with you over time.

You can estimate how many people left without providing feedback by comparing the total number of unique survey responses you received with the total number of customers that left your firm. It is logical to assume that these customers had negative experiences as well.

The most effective business strategy of all is a satisfied customer.

7. Follow-up polls

As mentioned above, surveys are an excellent way to measure customer satisfaction. The fact they record the customer's quick response to the brand encounter; follow-up surveys are very successful. After a protracted sales conversation or a challenging support situation, you will instantly understand how the customer is feeling.

You can utilize a few different kinds of follow-up surveys to determine the opinions of your customers.

Chapter 10

ENGAGEMENT OF THE CUSTOMER.

The emotional bond between a customer and a brand is known as customer engagement. Highly engaged customers are encouraged to spend more money, spread the word more, and show more loyalty. Your customer engagement plan must include delivering a superior customer experience.

Customer engagement is crucial because it benefits your brand by forging closer and more enduring ties with your customers. It keeps track of customer and business loyalty.

Customer engagement techniques help you establish a connection with customers, inform, keep an eye on, engage with, and create a solid base for your business.

The most effective business strategy of all is a satisfied customer.

Customer engagement is crucial for you since it enables them to organize customer segments for offering a tailored experience through different channels and permit omnichannel customer communication (across email, social media, live chat, etc.).

TYPES OF CUSTOMER ENGAGEMENT.

1. Contextual Engagement

Technology that enables marketers to comprehend a specific customer's behavior both historically and currently makes contextual engagement possible. "Engagement" is meaningless in isolation. Marketers can utilize this knowledge to further their objectives about the brand, the hour of the day, their location, their past, and other profile-related factors.

A more fulfilling individual experience is the end outcome. For instance, based on their past purchases, brands and merchants can send customers coupons or push a special offer to them via in-store notifications.

The most effective business strategy of all is a satisfied customer.

2. Use at Your Convenience.

The recently released Amazon Dash Button is the ideal illustration of this kind of engagement. Customers can utilize this button wherever they keep or use specific products like domestic appliances. When they run out, they merely press it, and, almost like magic, they receive the necessary things from Amazon at their door by enabling customers to quickly accept a new order for a specific product without having to leave their homes, leaving their houses to make their lives more convenient. Because it is simple, customers s will participate.

Any interaction that makes things more convenient gives the brand or retailer's systems the ability to learn more about the specific requirements, buying patterns, and preferences of each customer triggers and price points that might be utilized to increase the worth of that transaction to strengthen the impulse to purchase (emotionally, monetarily, and contextually).

The most effective business strategy of all is a satisfied customer.

3. Emotional Engagement.

It is frequently forgotten that emotions are the primary force behind engagement and loyalty. Given that people are emotional beings, providing customers with contextual relevance and convenience helps to reinforce the emotional worth they implicitly place in a brand.

Customer brand purchases, except for aspirational brands, are made in 99 percent of cases based on other unconscious emotional factors. These emotional ties have traditionally been restricted to either personal memories and experiences or marketing colors, pictures, and content. Marketers had no access to this form of engagement's more intimate elements because, even if you had that data, there was no way to comprehend or act upon any insight.

A good system monitors millions of data points that collectively form a very particular image of an individual's optimal environment for making decisions on what to buy, when, and how, customer-management technology enables this insight on a 1:1 basis at scale.

The most effective business strategy of all is a satisfied customer.

4. Social Interaction.

Success is determined by how well we interact with others. If the aforementioned are consistent with an individual, social advocacy, or the Mecca for most brands, is the immediate outcome? I've got more influence than any other marketer on the purchasing decisions of my network, or what is now referred to as influencer marketing. It's so simple for me to share positive brand experiences on my social media platforms, which encourages other people to look into the brand themselves.

This contact is largely about conversations that take place before and following a purchase and has little to do with the actual transaction. Understanding the many forms of customer interaction and having the technology in place to interpret the flood of data points to produce a more 1:1 experience. Creating and cultivating that vital customer relationship requires a positive engagement experience.

Gaining your customers' support is the best benefit of customer engagement.

The most effective business strategy of all is a satisfied customer.

CUSTOMER FEEDBACK.

You can gain valuable insights on how to raise customer satisfaction by paying close attention to what your customers have to say. But to guarantee that this information is put to use, you must compile a report on customers' feedback and distribute it to your teams and stakeholders.

Customer feedback refers to how people feel about your brand management, such as your service or product. The customer's report detailing their experience and level of satisfaction with your business.

You can organize the major outcomes of your feedback analysis and pinpoint the most important areas for improvement using a customer feedback report. Its major objective is to measure customer satisfaction and offer useful information for business growth.

The most effective business strategy of all is a satisfied customer.

In other words, it aids in measuring and assessing how successfully you are exceeding customers' expectations.

How to Write a Report on Customer Feedback.

It is preferable for you to:
- Recognize the demands and difficulties faced by your customers
- Identify crucial areas for development (and define the main priorities).
- Give internal teams data-driven insights so they can take action.
- Establish objectives and goals

Different feedback from your customers can include:

1. Positive feedback: This is a positive review of your product or service; customers in these categories are likely to stick with you and recommend you to others.

2. Negative report: This is an adverse, unfavorable, and in opposition to a good response. The report that, if caution is not exercised, tends to result in customer loss.

3. Null report: In this case, some customers provide no reviews or reports at all, which may not be helpful for the customer feedback survey. Customer engagement is crucial because of this. Companies can use customer feedback analysis to generate unique customer profiles for a variety of purposes and generate reports for every group:

- Calculate customer satisfaction (customer support team and stakeholders)
- Recognize user experience (product development team)
- Assess the effectiveness of customer service (customer support team)
- Find fresh business prospects (marketing and sales)

The most effective business strategy of all is a satisfied customer.

• Consider what you hope to learn from your customer feedback data, and keep in mind that the aims of your total business should be connected with your goals, which should be measurable.

There may also be a "Background section" in this initial section of your report where you briefly:
• Describe your company's present state and highlight any recent advancements.
• Describe the data collection process.
• Describe the specifics of your sample as well as the methods used to gather customer feedback.

Customer reviews offer a lot of quantifiable, measurable knowledge. These details are available from:
• Product reviews with star ratings
• Likes and shares on social media

- Responses to closed-ended questionnaires, such as multiple-choice and rating scale questions (NPS surveys or Customer Satisfaction surveys).

- Excel and other data analysis software make it simple to combine and evaluate quantitative data.

The significance of customer feedback.
One of the most crucial things a company can do to increase customer retention and foster brand loyalty is to listen to its customers when they provide feedback.

You may learn what keeps your devoted customers coming back by using customer feedback tools like your customer support statistics and customer satisfaction surveys. You can also learn what you can do to help convert a potential customer into a happy, new customer.

Customer feedback is the key to unlocking the useful insight you need to make it happen, and when these efforts are combined, they can have long-lasting effects that support your organization for years to come.

VARIOUS CUSTOMER FEEDBACK EVALUATIONS.

1. Customer comments

For enhanced customer insight, pay attention to what your customers are saying. These are the kinds of feedback that your customers voluntarily submit without being asked or prodded to do so:

a) Tickets for support

In most cases, customer support tickets serve as the primary means of communication between your company and its customers. Anytime a customer has a query, wants to offer a suggestion, or reports a problem, they submit a support ticket through one of the numerous channels you make available to them.

One benefit of using help desk software to manage your customer care tickets is that it enables you to add tags to each ticket, allowing you to highlight frequent product feedback and the features of your product that receive the most tickets (and are likely the least intuitive to customers and are therefore probably the least intuitive to your customers).

Furthermore, by utilizing the analytics features offered by your help desk software, you can create product feedback that is suitable and reliable.

It may be challenging to ensure that everyone consistently tags the same kinds of issues with the same tags in large teams. Sometimes a suggestion is seen as a bug by one person but as a UX issue by another, who may subsequently mark it as a feature request.

To ensure the accuracy of the compiled insights you receive from the tags, teach your customer service personnel to adhere to the tagging criteria.

The most effective business strategy of all is a satisfied customer.

Customer Satisfaction (CSAT) scores and the number of tickets for each feedback type tag, such as feature requests, the type of issue reported, and so forth, are the customer feedback metrics we monitor. We also consider how tags have changed throughout time.

b) Customer calls

Use the same tagging method for your phone support discussions that you do for tickets. If your help desk software does not already include an integrated phone channel, you will need to administrate the feedback form and analyze the data separately from the other support tickets you receive.

How you evaluate the feedback you receive from customers on your phone line could be substantially different, for instance, depending on whether you offer phone support to all of your customers or just your Enterprise customers.

The volume of these requests will be lower compared to support tickets received via your other channels if you just provide phone assistance to a small set of customers because customer feedback metrics track the number of feature requests, bug reports, and so on.

However, given that they can be your most valuable customers, you should make an effort to more readily available input that conveys its value based on economic impact rather than volume.

c) Outgoing communication

You might also use your outgoing communications to gather feedback. Every time you distribute a marketing newsletter, an onboarding email, or display an in-app message to your customers, you may provide them the chance to respond with comments or be directed to your website or help center. In either case, it's essential to transmit these messages through a platform that keeps track of these customer interactions. The open and click-through rates as well as the total number of responses are interesting indicators.

The most effective business strategy of all is a satisfied customer.

Ideally, this program will also let you specify and track goals for each communication you send rate of completion. You may set goals like encouraging customers to use a new feature or sign up for a particular plan.

You should target a certain group of your clientele using this strategy. For instance, if you recently released a new feature and want to see how your users are utilizing it, you can specifically target those who have used it by sending an email to your whole client base.

2. Customer feedback can be requested.

Become an expert in this process to access customer information. You request the following types of customer feedback specifically:

- CSAT (customer satisfaction) scores
- NPS (Net Promoter Score) polls
- Email newsletter responses
- Onboarding comments

- Customer testimonials
- Product evaluations
- Reactions from discussions of support
- Personal encounters such as focus groups

As with outgoing communications, survey opinion gathering can be obtrusive and your customers may occasionally consider it to be bothersome. Consequently, you ought to consider the method you use.

Make sure your feedback form is set up so you can gather insightful customer input data.

Additionally, if you use surveys, be ready and willing to engage in a discussion with your customers once they have given you, their feedback. It's poor customer service and a possible torpedo to contentment if after spending time providing feedback and inquiries only to never get a response, it's a frustrating experience.

The most effective business strategy of all is a satisfied customer.

A customer feedback survey can yield useful input when carried out properly. It may enable you to comprehend your customers more.

Chapter 11

HEALTH AND SAFETY OF CUSTOMERS.

The act of making sure that someone or something is preserved, protected, and secured is known as safety. To keep your customers safe, customer safety is crucial.

Customer service, safety, and quality are all crucial factors that all businesses ought to consider. Each of these elements has several significant downsides as well as management strategies.

It has been discovered that these three elements are somehow interconnected to one another to encourage improved performance. This is because the company will be able to boost performance. More customers result from better performance, and more customers result from more expectations for quality service and effective safety management.

The most effective business strategy of all is a satisfied customer.

For them to feel secure and, at the same time, more inclined to return in the future, all of these expectations must be met. Therefore, a warning sign must always be there to protect your customers from damage. **Safety for customers is crucial for all organizations.**

Customers must experience safety while making a purchase or while awaiting the completion of a service. Various kinds of safety policies can be put in place to guarantee the security of customers while a firm is carrying out transactions.

1. Place Markers.
There should be enough signage posted around the store or work area to highlight any potential hazards while making purchases or awaiting assistance. Place the signs in clearly accessible places where others can view them, like beside doorways.

For instance, shops with sliding glass doors should have signs on the entry and exit doors informing customers that they are automatic and that if the sensor doesn't detect movement, it can close on them. Repair services should put notices on the walls of the service garage indicating that customers are not allowed to enter the waiting area because of the large, constantly operating gear.

2. Fix Damages Right Away.

Repairing damage as soon as possible should be a rule that all businesses follow to prevent injuries to customers as they browse or wait for service. Damages include electrical outlet problems, broken shelves, water leaks, loose flooring, etc.

Employees must document any damage to the workplace and alert a manager as soon as possible. Attempting to repair the damage themselves or hiring a qualified handyman who is trained to repair any harm that may need fixing. A customer may file a claim if they are hurt because the damage is not repaired and cost the business money due to accidents and lawsuits.

The most effective business strategy of all is a satisfied customer.

3. Customers Should Be Alerted and Assist During an Emergency.

In an emergency, customers should leave the store or service area, a fire. All staff members should alert customers of emergencies and help them out of the shop in a timely and safe manner. The entire shop or service area has to be checked to make certain that no customers were forgotten. Doors should have signs identifying exits for emergencies.

4. Utilize tools to avoid mishaps.

Naturally, customers browse numerous retail establishments or wait long in service departments. Employees should use the company's safety equipment to indirectly avert an accident from happening to a customer, or admit that a spill has happened in an aisle. Never leave a ladder open or unattended. If a ladder is left unattended, a child or shopper might be lured to ascend the ladder. When not in use, the ladders should be closed and put firmly on the shelf using rubber straps made especially for holding ladders erect in a vertical position.

The most effective business strategy of all is a satisfied customer.

Customers should be warned of spills on the ground with yellow or orange caution cones until the spills can be cleared up, and ensure that the cones are placed in the middle of the spill. The customers will be safe while waiting or shopping thanks to these policies.

5. Help Customers Carry Heavy and Big Items.

Simply by lifting a large or heavy thing, customers risk injury. Employers must assist with products sold by retailers that are large and heavy, such as kitchen wares or furniture. Have a group of staff stroll about the shop to assist before customers attempt to move heavier goods themselves.

The assistance of customers can be provided without strain with effective employee coordination lifting something heavy. Additionally, shoppers should be provided with hand trucks and carts. For instance, if a customer is observed wandering around with a large cookware set, an employee should offer the customer a shopping cart to relieve them of the burden.

The most effective business strategy of all is a satisfied customer.

Your responsibility as a customer service expert is to ensure customer security. This entails managing what is produced or provided to your customers s as well as providing guidance, oversight, coordination, and management. You must keep an eye on how things are being produced for your customers.

Benefits of Protecting Customer Safety.

• Better standing with partners and suppliers

• The diminished risk of legal action

• Greater productivity as a result of happier, healthier, and more motivated workers.

• An improvement in the standing of corporate social responsibility among customers, investors, and communities.

SECURITY CAUSES MORE WORK.

A business's whole operation is impacted by a strong safety culture. When a business proves that safety is prioritized in the culture, which fosters participation in the workplace. Additionally, that setting may have an impact on improved communication in other workplace settings and an increase in output. Customers notice a clear connection between an organization's productivity and customer service.

For many customers, key employees like account executives are the first point of contact.

Customers may see through their activities that safety is a regular component of the workplace culture at their organization. Additionally, a strong safety culture might affect how customers view a company.

The most effective business strategy of all is a satisfied customer.

Reliability is a crucial component of daily operations. When a client is unsure of a provider's dependability, they are frequently less likely to choose to employ them and use their services. Contracting decisions and ultimately the bottom line can be influenced by knowing the service provider has a strong safety program that is ingrained in the company culture.

Beyond the firm, a safety culture must exist. Customers will return to a service provider who shows they care about their safety as much as their own. A business is unlikely to recover from an injury due to unsafe practices, items, or venues, regardless of how excellent the customer service team is, how attentive they are, or how smoothly the service or product delivery works.

The company's leadership must ultimately desire a robust safety culture. It is mostly the lack of desire that affects safety, it is not a result of a lack of money, resources, or time.

The most effective business strategy of all is a satisfied customer.

A successful safety in customer service is directly impacted by culture, or at the very least, trustworthiness and responsiveness, which affects customer satisfaction and eventually their financial situation.

Safety of the customer service representative.
First, there is internal customer/employee health and safety, but as an employee in the company, it is the responsibility of the human resources department to keep an eye on you and others.

You will receive training in your brand's health and safety policies and procedures.

To prevent injury, make sure you adhere to and observe all laws to ensure that you won't get hurt by customers.

The most effective business strategy of all is a satisfied customer.

What you must do if a customer approaches you with dangerous objects.

1. Leave the area right away.

Even though there is such a thing as self-defense, never stay to retaliate as it can eventually result in a bad situation.

2. Call Security's attention.

When you detect a customer coming toward you with potentially dangerous materials, leave immediately and report the situation to the proper personnel.

4. Exclude such visitors from the service area.

An aggressive customer can be requested to leave the property and asked not to return; thus, the business should think about banning them. The safety of everyone depends on it.

The most effective business strategy of all is a satisfied customer.

3. You should consider handing such individuals to office security.

Remember to serve them well with everything you have been taught and an amazing CSR attitude because "The Customer" is your boss, but when the scenario is growing chaotic, make sure of your safety. Be cautious as you play your part with aggressive clients.

Chapter 12

SELF-EVALUATION IN CUSTOMER SERVICE.

An intentional analysis of your work performance about how you serve your customers can be done through customer service self-evaluation. While your manager may give you a separate review, a self-evaluation draws on your perception and insight in addition to facts and customer feedback.

Self-performance reviews, also known as self-evaluations, are assessments of a person's strengths and flaws.

When people finish their self-evaluations, they are typically asked to list their proudest accomplishments, times when they met or exceeded their goals, situations in which they expanded their skill set, and any potential skill gaps.

These evaluations typically encompass a particular performance review report period, such as a quarter or a year.

The most effective business strategy of all is a satisfied customer.

ADVANTAGES OF SELF-EVALUATION IN CUSTOMER SERVICE

The benefits of self-evaluation are numerous for both businesses and employees.

- It enables managers to remain aware of the accomplishments and capabilities of their staff.
- It facilitates the evaluation of an employee's contribution.
- It encourages workers to accept responsibility for both their talents and flaws.
- It enables workers to showcase their successes.

Guidelines for drafting a self-evaluation report.

A key objective of the self-evaluation is to recognize your successes and recall the milestones in your development as a professional.

- Constantly work to improve.
- Act responsibly.
- Keep a record of your successes.
- Be critical and truthful.

The most effective business strategy of all is a satisfied customer.

It is important to deal with areas where your customer service self-evaluation is lacking It can be challenging to discuss your shortcomings or in challenging situations where you have acted badly. But correcting your flaws in your self-evaluations demonstrates that you accept responsibility for your errors and have a growth mentality.

Addressing your area of weakness gives you a basis for self-evaluation and enables you to ask your manager for help when you want to make improvements.

Following these three stages will help you enhance any area you have determined that needs work on your assessment of yourself:

1. Commit to getting better by admitting your shortcomings and stating that you wish to fix them.
2. You should set SMART goals for yourself because they must be timely, relevant, specified, measurable, and achievable.

The most effective business strategy of all is a satisfied customer.

3. After deciding to improve and setting a SMART goal, make an action plan on how you intend to carry it out.

There are many resources available that can assist you in figuring things out and you can also consider the following:

- A mentor with professional experience in your field.
- Books and podcasts about business.
- Free and affordable online courses.
- Peer coaching or one-on-one coaching.

Ask your family or friends for helpful suggestions if you can't seem to locate an answer that will work for you. Alternatively, ask your supervisors for help. Your opportunity to participate in your performance evaluation is supposed to be a discussion and collaboration to identify solutions.

The most effective business strategy of all is a satisfied customer.

PRIMARY AREAS TO INCLUDE IN YOUR SELF-EVALUATION

1. What to keep doing:

   - What actions have you taken that have helped you achieve your goals?
   - What has aided you in creating enduring business relationships?

2. What you should quit doing:

   - What are you doing that hurts how your peers or how your manager evaluates your performance?

3. What to start doing:

   - What should you be doing right now that you are not doing yet?

When you can respond to these inquiries, you are prepared to create your self-evaluation repo.

Customer service teamwork.

To achieve functional, social, and emotional customer pleasure as well as greater sales, loyalty, and retention for the business, collaboration in customer service is crucial. Consequently, every division of a brand's customer service must work together to realize all of these objectives.

There are many customer service divisions and it varies depending on brands.

Here is a list of some:

1. Team for live chat.
2. On-call group.
3. Data management team for clients.
4. Email Group.

5. Technical assistance group.
6. Team for loyalty and retention.
7. Coordinating Group.

And a large number of other divisions depending on the business.

For each of the aforementioned teams, there is a sub-team lead for each section. However, there is only one TEAM LEADER KNOWN AS THE HEAD OF CUSTOMER SERVICE IN A COMPANY, who may have an assistant.

THE RESPONSIBILITIES OF A CUSTOMER SERVICE HEAD OR DIRECTOR.

Working in customer service requires being ready to handle challenging situations right away. When something goes wrong, the agent always calls their customer service manager first, whether in person, over the phone, or by email. Customer service heads manage the ticket backlog, enhance the structure, assist teams in exceeding performance targets, and maintain a high level of customer satisfaction.

It is managing people that is more crucial. The difference between a team that provides a memorable customer experience and one that merely responds to inquiries from customers can be made by a skilled customer service head.

While some traits are required of every customer care representative, a manager can be distinguished from others by having a few additional talents. Here is a list of abilities you must possess if you want to work as a customer service head or director:

1. Motivating Your Staff

Without exception, this is the most critical ability that every manager should possess no matter the department. Effective managers understand how to maintain their own and their teams' motivation.

You should, as a manager, capitalize on your team's advantages. Additionally, how you feel about your team will significantly influence their work atmosphere.

You must support your colleagues and lend a helping hand when necessary. They would have a sense of belonging because of your trust and respect, which would lead to higher performance.

The most effective business strategy of all is a satisfied customer.

2. Educating Your Staff

Giving your employees the necessary training is the greatest approach to ensure that they are prepared for their roles and are ready to carry out the instruction given to them. The instruction they receive ought to enable them to give your customers a fantastic experience. Ask them if they are experiencing any problems at work and provide timely feedback.

Plan professional development training sessions for the new team members to enhance their skills. Ask their agents what they would want to learn if you are unsure of where to start. Below are some queries to get their perspective:

- What is the most difficult aspect of your job?

- What one aspect of our team would you like to see improved?

- Do you believe that the team needs to interact more?

- What steps would you propose taking to improve team chemistry?

3. Managing Your Workflow

The duties of a customer service manager include leading meetings, handling challenging issues, suggesting ways to provide better customer service, and directing everyone on your team. Additionally, you would need to make crucial and tough decisions that could be fairly stressful. However, not all issues are equal, so you must choose which to address first. An arrangement that enables you to make the most of your time is what you require.

4. Monitor Performance

Monitoring the performance of your staff is essential for assessing the level of customer service. While metrics based on the performance of agents, such as response time and resolution time, comparative team-based indicators like the satisfaction score and contact ratio show how each member is performing in a general summary. Even though metrics are a common technique to monitor performance, don't rely too heavily on them even if your staff is working remotely, make it a practice to communicate with everyone frequently.

The most effective business strategy of all is a satisfied customer.

Even the team that works remotely, makes it a routine to communicate with each team frequently and assist them if they encounter any difficulties.

5. Dealing with De-escalations

There will be instances where the customer will state, "I need you to contact your manager" despite your team's best efforts. This is a blatant sign that the customer is dissatisfied and if they don't get the refund or warranty extension they requested, they will churn. In situations like these, think about your options and decide what will work best for you and the customer. Talk with them, take a decision, and put the best de-escalation strategy into action.

6. Increasing Performance

The demands of your customers are increasing, so you need to make sure that your team is prepared to take charge of them. Examine the way your department is running critically to see if anything needs to be changed.

The most effective business strategy of all is a satisfied customer.

Even though a change is for the better, people will still be resistant to it. So, make sure you have the numbers to back up your claim and explain how the adjustment will benefit them. Suppose your agents are unable to provide service from a single mailbox as a result of rising customer problems; it is either the resolution is delayed or it is missed altogether. Customers and your team are both frustrated, therefore adding more representatives would only make things more confusing. Look for a help desk that would reduce stress in a circumstance like this, thereby encouraging your group to work together more effectively and resolve conflicts more quicker abilities.

7. Re-evaluating Techniques.

Considering how many businesses use the standard of their customer service as a brand differentiator, email replies alone are no longer sufficient. An approach to customer service that offers great assistance, and strong customer retention and support is a requirement these days. Investigate new opportunities and ways to personalize customer service.

The most effective business strategy of all is a satisfied customer.

Consider the long term and try out prospects for upselling and cross-selling. In any case, every manager should have a plan and a strategy in mind.

A critical strategic and operational leadership position is that of the director or manager of customer service, accountable for creating, delivering, and ensuring the quality of customer service

and the deliberate formulation of technological, procedural, and operational requirements, to achieve important customer service outcomes in a B2B (business to business) or B2C (business to customer) setting. Significant degrees of operational accountability and responsibility are part of the role and abilities delivery.

Identification and development of all cultures, process and performance upgrades, as well as customer and employee efficiency, directing and training a workforce that often conducts customer encounters across several channels, including the front and back offices, telephone, email, online, live chat, video, and social media, are the responsibilities of the Customer Service Director.

The most effective business strategy of all is a satisfied customer.

Develop a senior operational management team through strategic leadership to improve by establishing precise, accountable performance measures.

To support this further, your background and abilities as a director or manager must include the following:
- In charge of budgets for the profit and loss or cost center/profit center.
- Establish a culture and procedures that help the company achieve its goals and objectives in terms of customer service.
- Boost CSAT (Customer Satisfaction), NPS (Net Promoter Score), or another Customer metric.
- A decrease in the cost of serving.
- Engage and empower the team by providing customer service.
- Improving First Call Resolution.
- Discover new tools and technology to enhance customer service.
- Increase sales through superior service.

The most effective business strategy of all is a satisfied customer.

- Use root cause analytics and customer insight to find company-wide improvements to the Board/Senior Stakeholder Peers, and deliver them.
- Represent the customer's voice throughout the organization.
- Recognizing and giving feedback using personal development and effective plans and chances for coaching and development are provided.
- Responsible for ensuring that all legal and regulatory obligations are met.
- The detection of any possible danger problems.
- Specify, discuss, and reach an agreement on the efficient use of resources in line with the service working with, overseeing, or
being in charge of necessary resource planning in coordination with the company's goals and SLAs.
- Effectively collaborate with all peers, the board, and stakeholders in commercial and financial matters to negotiate and encourage customer improvements, using marketing and operations.
- Constantly create upgrades and integrate effective change initiatives.

The most effective business strategy of all is a satisfied customer.

- Promote consistency and quality.
- Collaborate with customer relationships to maximize current customers' commercial success, teamwork, planning, and expanded revenue streams.

You must have the following experience to qualify as a Customer Service Team head:

- Significant management experience with operational customer service teams.
- A strong strategic emphasis on the needs of the client and an awareness of the larger issues affecting the pertinent markets
- Demonstrated management and/or relationship management expertise in a senior, strategic role.
- Proven track record of surpassing goals, KPIs, and SLAs in a quality-driven, law-abiding workplace
- Capable of strategizing, developing recommendations, and interpreting MI (management information) and BI (business intelligence).
- Exhibit the capacity to inspire and interact with people at all levels.

The most effective business strategy of all is a satisfied customer.

- Capable of delivering service improvements by utilizing these partnerships.
- Strong negotiating and communication abilities.
- Capable of adjusting to change and thriving in it.
- A demonstration of strong leadership abilities.

How to resolve disputes between team members.
Because of our diverse personalities, backgrounds, viewpoints, and attitudes. There could miscommunication between team members and they can be handled by:
- Paying close attention to both sides.
- Paying attention to actions and circumstances rather than people.
- Listing areas where you and others disagree.
- Giving the regions of contention priority.
- Creating a strategy to address each conflict.
- Implementing your plan as intended.
- Offering remedies depending on the disagreement or miscommunication.

- Explaining to them the value of the company's objective and how a disagreement can detract from it.
- Making sure the apology is proper.
- Leading them on a journey of love and cooperation.
- Expanding on your achievement.

How to inspire and motivate your team members to work toward the same objective.
- Talk to them at lunchtime, if possible.
- Organize a Picnic.
- Encourage them by taking them to conferences and training sessions for customer service.
- frequently keep an eye on them
- Make sure that their health and safety come first.
- Issue rewards, data subscriptions, and presents for representatives or sub-team heads.
- Make sure they are also promoted.
- Encourage them.
- Plan the celebration for the end of the quarter or year.
- Instill in them a passion for labor.

The most effective business strategy of all is a satisfied customer.

Duties of a customer service agent

1. Be as focused as your leader
2. Pay close attention to all rules.
3. Follow the lead of your sub-team.
4. Move in love.
5. Decrease backbiting
6. Be knowledgeable, accountable, and responsible.
7. Execute your assignment skillfully and successfully.
8. Turn in your assignment by the deadline.
9. Accept reprimands.
10. Arrive early for meetings or the office.
11. Support your boss and the corporate objective.
12. Accept cooperation as yours.

How to deal with disagreements among team members.

1. Pay close attention to the other party.
2. Move in love.
3. Negotiate a fair settlement.
4. If it is getting out of hand, report it to your sub-team lead who is a higher authority.

The most effective business strategy of all is a satisfied customer.

Don't be the reason your team's objectives aren't met, be on the same page as your teams. In the future, when you are expanding your portfolio, you will be a good leader in customer service if you are a good customer representative today.

As the head of customer service, it is your responsibility to manage the customer and your service team.

Regarding the Team, it includes the following:

1. People of various personalities get along together.
2. Individuals with various perspectives.
3. Individuals from various backgrounds.
4. People with various viewpoints.

To reach the same project viewpoint or view, they get together with the same perspective, a common history, and a specific goal in mind towards the conclusion of their task, with their varied perspectives on a certain issue. All team members must be observing and moving toward;

1. the same way
2 Achieving that one objective.

The most effective business strategy of all is a satisfied customer.

The following must be done to accomplish this SAME GOAL:

1. Work together

2. Work collaboratively

3. Share endeavors

4. Cooperate.

5. Pay Attention, to both mental and emotional capacity (passion)

7. Support each other.

8. Obedience

In Summary.

The customer is also your bank account, not simply a king. Ruining a customer's experience can bring down your bank. Your error will propagate thanks to one furious customer. One customer can ruin your company, while a different customer can provide you with millions of referrals.

Even if they seem unreasonable, resist the want to snap at them or act aggressively. Send them your love. Learn how to win customers' loyalty and keep them.

The most effective business strategy of all is a satisfied customer.

Success is in your hands; use it. How far you want to go is entirely up to you. Be great whenever you are a member of a group.

The most effective business strategy of all is a satisfied customer.

Chapter 13

POLICY FOR CUSTOMER SERVICE.

A customer service policy is a document or model that directs how your staff and your business handle customer service. Most companies are aware of how important customer service is to their success. You need an excellent customer service policy to provide effective customer service. Empowering your staff is the finest method for enabling them to excel in customer service. With empowered personnel, it can be challenging to maintain uniform customer care throughout the company; for this reason, customer service policies are necessary.

For instance, your staff members must be aware of the limits of what they can do to satisfy customers and keep them coming back.

Although many businesses make their rules publicly available to allow customers to know what kind of high-quality service they can anticipate, this is sometimes merely an internal code of conduct. The expectations of customers have increased significantly. Consistency is one of those demands. Regardless of the channel they use, the customer care agent, they speak to, or the location they visit, customers expect a consistent experience.

Brands that provide consistent in-store and online experiences will attract more customers than those whose offerings are uneven. You must establish rules if you want all of your staff to deliver a consistent level of service. Your customer service policy is intended to address this.

The most effective business strategy of all is a satisfied customer.

IMPORTANCE OF CUSTOMER SERVICE POLICY.

A company that prioritizes its customers must have customer service rules to:

1. Clarify your objectives:

You have objectives for customer service at your company. They might involve things like offering prompt customer service or being kind and understanding. A customer service policy links those broad objectives to specific actions that your staff members should follow. It is clear in the policy that responding to a customer within an hour or a week equates to rapidly resolving an issue.

2. Keep everyone in the office informed:

Everyone is on the same page when there is a customer service policy. With so many teams switching to remote work, this is becoming more and more crucial. In the future, about 85% of customer service leaders may likely adopt remote or hybrid operating methods.

The most effective business strategy of all is a satisfied customer.

3. Point out significant benchmarks:

Your customer service policy includes critical rules on other crucial procedures including collaboration and escalation, as well as benchmarks for response and resolution times. You can use the criteria for excellent service outlined in the policy when assessing the performance of your agents and team.

4. Improve the level of customer service your team provides.

Employees are less inclined to take shortcuts when they are clear on what is expected of them. There is no space for debate over what constitutes excellent customer service. Customers will know what to expect if you choose to make your customer service policy public. You may, for instance, mention your return policy or list the products that are guaranteed.

HOW TO CREATE A POLICY FOR CUSTOMER SERVICE

Taking the big picture into account is the first step in developing a customer service policy. Mission statements are a common starting point for customer service rules.

This often contains one or two lines that succinctly state how you intend to handle your customers. The main vision is stated in the mission statement. Here are three things to consider when you draft the supporting guidelines:

1. Know what your customers require.

Your customer service policy should take into account the actual requirements and demands of your customers. Research instead of assuming.

Speak to your customer service staff first. They are already very familiar with the frequent problems and worries of customers.

The most effective business strategy of all is a satisfied customer.

To find out more about what your customers desire and what irritates them, you may also send out customer surveys. Consider including language in the policy to address issues like their dissatisfaction with the speed of service or the regularity of their interactions with your business.

2. Know what to offer your customers.

It may sound wonderful to promise your customers anything they desire, but your customer service policy needs to be realistic about what you can deliver. If the promises made in the document can't be kept, both your staff and your customers s will find it meaningless.

3. Learn how your team is doing right now.

If you're not satisfied with the service, you can now, think about your technology. What you can guarantee is significantly impacted by your customer service software. Know the typical response time for you, the number of tickets you handle each month, the methods available for customers to reach you, and set ambitious yet attainable objectives.

The most effective business strategy of all is a satisfied customer.

CONTENTS IN CUSTOMER SERVICE POLICY.

Guidelines for how your customer care agents will behave in particular situations should make up the majority of your customer service policy. Although they will be specific to your company, there are some general items to think about.

1. Your company's values:

You might include these in your mission statement for customer service.

2. Timeframe for reaction and resolution:

In an hour or six, when will you respond to your customers? How quickly do you fix problems? What time do you provide support?

3. Standards of professionalism:

How should your staff act while interacting with customers? For face-to-face conversations, this might also include standards for appropriate attire. Expectations for how remote customer support representatives greet and converse with customers may be included also.

The most effective business strategy of all is a satisfied customer.

4. Business or industry-specific regulations:

If you own an online store, for instance, you might include the policies for shipping, returns, exchanges, and billing.

5. Channels for gathering criticism:

Include the method and frequency of collection. Inform customers how to contact you and how you will handle unfavorable comments if your customer service policy is customer-facing.

6. What to do if customers are dissatisfied:

Does the customer receive a refund if unsatisfied? How will the customer receive the refund?

7. The matrix of escalation:

Ensure that everyone is aware of what to do if these rules or SLAs (service-level agreements) are broken.

The most effective business strategy of all is a satisfied customer.

8. Best practices for working with other teams:

How do you typically raise bug requests? What are reasonable waiting periods? How can delays from other departments be escalated?

Some suggestions for developing a customer service policy.

All customer service procedures are not created equal. Your policy needs to be impactful and unambiguous to get the best results. The following advice will assist you in creating the ideal policy:

• Be precise.

For instance, promising a 24-hour email response time is preferable to simply promising quick service.

• Keep it basic.

A page or two will do. Prioritize the objectives that will have the most influence on the experience of the customer.

• Make it simple to comprehend.

Your policy should be understandable to everyone who reads it, including customers and brand-new employees. That entails eliminating business and industrial jargon.

The most effective business strategy of all is a satisfied customer.

Putting the policy in place.

Your company's customer service policy should be available to every employee. It should be included in your internal knowledge base so that team members may immediately check it. Post hard copies in your businesses or working areas. Additionally, you can post it on your website for customers to read.

The policy should be covered in training for personnel in customer service. These are the top priorities for your team, so take the time to explain each one to your trainees.

Follow up on your success after putting your policy in place. You may monitor SLAs and CSAT using your helpdesk. If you aren't meeting the benchmarks outlined in your customer service policy, it may be a sign that your staff is underperforming or requires additional training.

It might also imply that, given your capabilities and technology, the rules are inapplicable. If the latter, find out what your team needs to accomplish its goals.

The most effective business strategy of all is a satisfied customer.

Customer service guidelines are dynamic documents. Create a plan to review the policy annually and update it if anything changes.

Technology for customer service and your policy.
Only when everyone has access to the same knowledge and resources can consistency in service be achieved. Consider your customer service policy's objectives when you assess new solutions. If you promise to answer to customers on many channels, for instance, make it simple for your agents to do so by selecting a platform that offers omnichannel support. SLAs can be monitored via your helpdesk. The criteria in your customer service policy should be met by these SLAs. Create reports to investigate breaches and identify their causes and patterns. An easy method to ensure that your company upholds a consistently high level is to establish a customer service policy.

Your customer service policy should include concepts that are based on your company's objectives and provide specific suggestions for how to get there.

The most effective business strategy of all is a satisfied customer.

The correct tools will make it simpler to adhere to the commitments stated in your customer service policy.

SUMMARY.

Customer service is the culmination of all that a firm does to satisfy customers and match their expectations. Because customer service goes beyond only offering a way to increase sales, it is crucial. It is also asserted that good customer service programs encourage repeat business from customers. A terrific experience offers exceptional value for the money. Simply put, if your customers are satisfied, your business will benefit as well, therefore getting customer service right is crucial. Happy customers are frequently brand loyal and are always prepared to make more purchases.

The most effective business strategy of all is a satisfied customer.

www.ingramcontent.com/pod-product-compliance
Lightning Source LLC
Chambersburg PA
CBHW052355220526
45465CB00003BA/1121